lonely planet

50

Places to Stay

TO BLOW YOUR MIND

Contents

Splurge // High-end luxury

Wonder // The totally unexpected

Introduction

You know that old adage 'it's about the journey not the destination'? Well, that just doesn't apply here. Each and every one of these spectacular places to stay is a destination in its own right, and each place is totally worth the journey. From glass igloos in Finnish Lapland to wooden spheres suspended in the treetops in Canada; geodesic domes in the Patagonian wilderness to old-school opulence at New York's Plaza Hotel; these are the ultimate in overnight experiences. Not every place is a budget buster; sometimes it's about the spectacular locations, like the gravity-defying Bivacco Gervasutti on Mont Blanc in Italy (page 50). There are places that literally disappear into their surroundings like the Mirrorcube in Harads, Sweden (page 42), and others that stand tall and command attention like the Frank Gehry-designed Hotel Marques de Riscal in Spain (page 92). We've only included a place if it gives us a thrill, opens our eyes, makes us catch our breath and inspires us to see the world through different eyes. We hope they make you smile, make you marvel, and that they motivate you to go on a journey to a new destination.

Elegant // Traditional opulence

Ashford Castle, County Mayo, Ireland

WE COULD GET USED TO THIS.

Who wouldn't be swept up in the fantasy of medieval castle life? Especially considering this place is now packed with modern five-star amenities.

THIS PLACE IS ENORMOUS.

Built in 1228 by Anglo-Normans, the castle has received numerous add-ons and extensions over the years, including a French-style chateau in 1715 and Victorian buildings by the then-owners, the Guinness family, in 1852. Nowadays it's a spectacular 83-room hotel with a cinema, spa, golf course, tennis courts, fishing, lake cruises, horse-riding, clay-shooting, archery, zip-lining, tree climbing, and of course, falconry. We're not even kidding.

WE DON'T KNOW WHERE TO START.

Considering the sumptuous, spacious and elegant design of the rooms and suites at the hotel it's amazing anyone makes it outside to partake in all the activities. Each room has been lovingly realised with antique furnishings, bespoke beds and carpets, chandeliers and one-of-a-kind works of art. There's 24-hour in-room dining available, an in-room bar, cable TV with on-demand movies, as well as deluxe toiletries and plush bathrobes and slippers. You will never want to leave.

LUKLA – SHYANGBOCHE MARG, KHUMJUNG 56000, NEPAL

HOTELEVERESTVIEW.COM

Hotel Everest View, Khumjung, Nepal

EVEREST FOR THE ARMCHAIR ENTHUSIASTS?

Or a reward for a life-long ambition achieved? Whichever way you choose to experience Hotel Everest View there's no denying the joy of combining views of the world's highest peak with world-class luxury.

SO WE CAN GET ALL THE GAIN FOR NONE OF THE PAIN?

The hotel has been listed by the Guinness Book of Records as the world's highest at 3880m so beware the dreaded altitude sickness. One way to avoid being struck down is to trek to the hotel from Lukla – the three-day hike gives guests the opportunity to slowly acclimatise as well as experience the magnificent scenery. Of course, if this just sounds like way too much work you can fly in on a helicopter from Kathmandu.

A HELICOPTER? THAT'S CHEATING!

If you hike the trail to the hotel you've definitely earned bragging rights and anyone who has choppered in should be forced to buy the first round of drinks to be consumed on the terrace. Then you're all free to enjoy one of the world's most stunning sights.

I AHWAHNEE DRIVE, YOSEMITE
NATIONAL PARK, CA 95389, UNITED STATES
WWW.TRAVELYOSEMITE.COM/LODGING

Majestic Hotel, Yosemite National Park, California, USA

CAN'T WE JUST PITCH A TENT HERE AND SOAK IN THE GRANDEUR?

There's no denying the major drawcards in Yosemite are the jaw-dropping natural wonders. Hiking, climbing and camping throughout this expansive and stunningly varied national park is an experience of a lifetime, but every now and again you just need a little luxury to go with the majesty.

OK, WE'VE PACKED AWAY OUR HIKING BOOTS AND DONNED OUR FINEST. BRING ON THE EXTRAVAGANCE.

The Majestic is all about old-school elegance. Built in 1927, the hotel showcases original paintings, rugs and tapestries from the period throughout the magnificent common spaces. The entrance hall features towering ceilings over 30 feet high, there's a chandelier-lit dining room and even a pool.

WE COULD GET SO COMFORTABLE HERE WE'D FORGET WHERE WE WERE.

Not likely. One of the most magnificent things about the Majestic is the nod of deference it gives to its unique location. The grand granite and pine façade proudly mirrors the imposing rock face of the surrounding mountains and the private rooms all open onto spectacular views of some of the park's most well known attractions, like Yosemite Falls and Half Dome.

AV. IGNACIO COL. CENTRO, RAYON 434, ZACATECAS CENTRO, 98000
ZACATECAS, ZAC., MEXICO. WWW.QUINTAREAL.COM/ZACATECAS-EN

Quinta Real Zacatecas, Zacatecas, Mexico

GOT TO SAY WE'RE FANS OF SEEING A BULLRING BEING MADE THE MOST OF WITHOUT THE BULLS.

Cleverly designed to maximise the drama of the 17th century San Pedro bullring, the hotel's rooms encircle the ring, recessed in the original colonial architecture. The hotel also overlooks the city's ancient arched viaduct.

SO THE BLOODSHED IS OVER, WHAT'S IN THE RING NOW?

Cocktails and canapes have replaced the one-time gory spectacle. A refined Mexican restaurant overlooks the ring and there's even a bar inside the former bull corrals.

AND OUR RINGSIDE SUITE? WHAT CAN WE EXPECT TO FIND THERE?

Expect to have no expense spared. The rooms are spacious and combine modern features like Jacuzzi baths and satellite TV, with colonial touches such as beds set back under stone archways to mirror the external archways of the bullring.

NOW WE KNOW WHAT IT'S LIKE TO BE SPOILED MEXICAN STYLE.

The silver mines of Zacatecas brought untold wealth to the city and now the Quinta Real Zacatecas gives its guests the opportunity to experience this old-time opulence and extravagance.

Trans-Siberian Express, Russia-Mongolia

A MOVING TARGET.

We're being a bit cheeky here by introducing a place to stay that's on the move, but sleeping aboard this legendary express is absolutely one for the bucket list. There is more than one itinerary on board a number of trains crossing the region, but we're talking about the classic Moscow to Vladivostok via Lake Baikal, the world's largest freshwater lake.

AND THE TRAINS THEMSELVES?

Banish thoughts of cramped bunk beds and queuing for the toilets – the Golden Eagle Luxury Trains set the standard for extravagance on rails. Choose from three different cabins: the

Imperial Suite; the Gold Cabin; and the Silver cabin – all cabins feature a private en suite bathroom, but in the Imperial Suite you'll get a king-sized bed and a bottle of Dom Perignon on arrival. Just saying.

AND IF WE CAN'T FORK OUT TO SLEEP LIKE ROYALTY?

Don't fret, the sumptuousness spreads to shared areas like the Bar Lounge Car with its rich, red armchairs, and the stunning dining car where the on-board chef spoils guests with Russian specialties like black sturgeon caviar.

Escape // Remote and secluded

Attrap Reves, Various Locations, France

WHAT DO YOU MEAN BY 'VARIOUS LOCATIONS'?

The concept of this place revolves around creating an at-one-with-nature experience that is outside the box. Or should we say outside the bubble. Attrap Reves provides its guests with their very own bubble to sleep in across six different locations throughout France.

EXCUSE ME, DID YOU SAY 'BUBBLE'?

We did indeed. The accommodation is a see-through bubble (well, it's kind of igloo shaped, but let's not quibble) furnished with a bed and small seating area. Each bubble is decorated differently, but every one is entirely exposed, giving guests a hard-to-beat view of the surrounding bush and, more spectacularly, the expansive night sky.

AGAIN, COMPLETELY SEE-THROUGH?

Don't go all shy on us now. It's nothing the local woodland creatures haven't seen before. The remoteness of the locations in which the bubbles are set up guarantees the privacy of anyone worried about indecent exposure. Instead it's about being as close to nature as possible without the stings, scratches, bites and itches. Sounds like a bright idea, right?

9057 WEISSBAD/AI, SWITZERLAND

AESCHER-AI.CH

Berggasthaus Aescher-Wildkirchli, Schwende District, Switzerland

THIS PLACE IS SURELY THE STUFF OF SWISS ALPINE DREAMS...

This magnificently situated guesthouse is quintessentially Swiss. The picture-postcard façade is all wooden angles and shuttered windows, while the body of the guesthouse backs into the spectacularly cleaved cliff-face of the Ebenalp Peak; the back wall of the guesthouse is actually the mountain itself. From the front there are expansive Alpine views stretching all the way to the remote Seealpsee Lake.

WHAT A SPECTACULAR SETTING.

This is definitely the fairy-tale version of Switzerland on show. The sleeping arrangements, however, may not be everyone's cup of kirsch. From its modest days as a mountain hut housing farmers and their goats and cows, the guesthouse has evolved to include shared dormitory accommodation, but no private lodgings.

THERE'S NOTHING LIKE SHARING SLEEPING QUARTERS TO GET THE PARTY STARTED.

That's the spirit. The communal-style sleeping arrangements lend themselves to good times and you'll have no trouble finding a friend to share a beer with after a long day of hiking in the mountains.

420 HORNE LAKE RD, QUALICUM BEACH, BC V9K 1Z7,
CANADA FREESPIRITSPHERES.COM

Free Spirit Spheres, Vancouver Island, Canada

SOUNDS LIKE WE'RE OFF ON A VOYAGE OF SELF-DISCOVERY.

We'll eat our hemp hat if you don't find peace sleeping inside one of these suspended spheres swaying gently in the treetops.

SOUL-SEARCHING ASIDE, THIS DOES SOUND LIKE A UNIQUE EXPERIENCE.

These snug spheres are the product of the creative and engineering mind of Tom Chudleigh, who aims for his guests to be able to commune with nature in a way they never have before – within the cosy confines of one of his three individually-named treetop orbs.

YOU'D BETTER INTRODUCE US TO THE ORBS THEN.

The first orb to take up residence in the canopy was Eve. Made of wood, she sleeps just one contemplative guest. Eryn came next; she's made of Sitka spruce and sleeps three (one in a loft bed); and the newest of the collective, Melody, the only orb to be made of a fibreglass exterior with a dark walnut interior, sleeps two. All the orbs are simply furnished with basic amenities like heating, fresh water, couches and beds. However, the most priceless amenity up here in the treetops is the peace and quiet.

Junk cruise, Ha Long Bay, Quang Ninh Province, Vietnam

A BOAT CRUISE? SHOULDN'T WE BE SAVING THAT FOR RETIREMENT?

Banish thoughts of bingo and 4pm dinners. Picture instead an amenity-packed private cabin replete with spa and up-close views of the spectacular karst formations that make up the UNESCO-listed Ha Long Bay.

IT'S SOUNDING SPECIAL NOW.

Each luxury boat that sails these waters comes with an experienced crew that caters to the culinary needs of guests on board. Lunches and dinners are extravagant banquet-style affairs showcasing traditional Vietnamese cuisine, often with a focus on local seafood. Come hungry.

AND DO WE GET A CHANCE TO GET UP CLOSE TO THE UNSPOILED WONDER OF THE BAY?

The itineraries for each cruise are slightly different but every one factors in some time for off-the-boat activities. Think kayaking around the karsts, visiting local floating fishing or oyster-farming villages, or exploring stunning caves like the colourfully-lit Sung Sot.

HOW LONG DO WE GET TO SOAK UP THE SERENITY?

Most travellers choose either the one- or two-night itinerary. There's only so much wonder one can take, right?

28

Kakslauttanen Arctic Resort, Finnish Lapland

GLASS IGLOOS IN REMOTE LAPLAND? SOUNDS LIKE THE STUFF OF FAIRY TALES.

We're going to go out on a snow-laden limb here and say that this place delivers one of earth's most magical experiences.

WHOAH, THAT'S A BIG CALL.

Picture this: it's dark outside, snow is gently falling, you're lying on your bed in your own private igloo as enormous Arctic pines frame the swirling, shifting kaleidoscopic majesty of the Northern Lights above you. Now tell us that's not otherworldly.

THIS IS SOUNDING PRETTY SPECIAL.

Add in the possibility of staying in a snow igloo where the inside hovers at a constant −3 to −6°C and you've got yourself some adventure to add to your luxury.

IF WE WANT TO VENTURE OUTSIDE OUR IGLOOS, WHAT CAN WE DO?

The resort borders the pristine Urho Kekkonen National Park, where you can hike through some of the world's most unspoiled wilderness. Oh, and did we mention Santa lives here? When he's not busy supervising the elves or tending to the reindeers he opens the doors of his home to intrepid travellers. Told you this place was magic.

Longitude 131, Uluru–Kata Tjuta National Park, Australia

NOT GIVING MUCH AWAY WITH THE NAME.
There's no mistaking the image though. Yes, that is Australia's world-famous and iconic landmark Uluru that you can see from your own private white-topped tent.

OH, SO WE'RE CAMPING IN THE DESERT?
Not exactly. There's no sagging canvas or dinky fly-nets here; this is next-level glamping. You'll be staying in one of only 15 luxuriously kitted-out tented cabins all positioned to make the most of the view of the serene and dramatic expanse of the Simpson Desert and the major drawcard, Uluru.

IT'S NOT OFTEN A HOLIDAY IN THE RED CENTRE TURNS INTO A TOP-END EXPERIENCE.
One of the most memorable things about a trip to Longitude 131 and Australia's vast outback is the connection the resort honours to the land and to the land's traditional custodians. Alongside the extravagant five-star features, the resort sports serious eco credentials and provides guests with the opportunity to learn about the centuries-old culture of the Anangu people. Listening to ancient creation stories as the sun sets over Uluru and Kata Tjuta (the Olgas) is an experience not soon forgotten.

SOLENT FORTS PORT OFFICE, CANALSIDE, GUNWHARF QUAYS, PORTSMOUTH, HAMPSHIRE, PO1 3FH, UK. WWW.SOLENTFORTS.COM/NO-MANS-FORT/

No Man's Fort, Solent, Portsmouth, UK

CHILDHOOD DREAMS REALISED – SLEEPING IN A FORT!

It's just as adventurous as it sounds and if you're in any doubt about its uniqueness just check out the myriad 'Most Unusual' lists the fort constantly features on. This hulking, iron-plated, Victorian citadel has long given up on its original assignment to protect Portsmouth from French attack, and after it slipped into disrepair for more than 50 years some bright spark had the idea to turn the crumbling, out-to-sea wreck into luxury accommodation. Well, of course they did.

THE WHOLE 'HULKING, IRON-PLATED' BIT DOESN'T EXACTLY SCREAM COMFORT.

Don't judge a fort by its cover. What if we say things like rooftop hot tubs, helipad, spa, and driving range stocked with biodegradable golf balls. Starting to feel a bit more comfortable now?

SOUNDING WEIRDER AND MORE WONDERFUL.

The spacious guestrooms are chic and luxuriously fitted out – nothing weird about it. Of course, if you want to spice things up a bit the Fort hosts regular themed parties which are garnering a big following and currently sell out weeks in advance.

144 ONE LOVE DRIVE, NEGRIL, JAMAICA
WWW.THECAVESHOTEL.COM

The Caves, Negril, Jamaica

WE'RE HAPPY TO RETURN TO OUR CAVEMAN ROOTS IF THIS IS WHERE WE GET TO STAY.

Making the most of the stunning natural scenery and cliff-side location, the Caves resort is an idyllic slice of beachside life. Shimmering below the 12 cliff-top cottages is the sparkly sapphire sea and only a few miles away there's Negril's bustling seven-mile beach.

WHERE DO THE CAVES COME INTO IT?

Over hundreds of years the elements have carved caves from the porous limestone cliffs. Many of the caves can be explored by boat down on the water, but if you're feeling lazy the resort will serve you a special meal in your very own private cave/dining room.

OK, WE'VE EVOLVED PAST CAVE DWELLING; WHAT'S OUR ROOM LIKE?

There's a choice of one-bedroom or two-bedroom suites/cottages – all surrounded by lush tropical vegetation and kitted out island-style with simple and colourful decor. If you really want to spoil yourself there's a private villa with its very own pool, Jacuzzi, sauna and more than half an acre of sequestered garden. It should go without saying that there's a spa for all.

55 MOO 5 TAMBOL WANGKRAJAE, AMPHUR SAIYOK, KANCHANABURI
71150, THAILAND. WWW.THEFLOATHOUSERIVERKWAI.COM

The FloatHouse River Kwai, Kanchanaburi, Thailand

FLOATING ON A HOUSE ON THE RIVER KWAI SOUNDS MORE FUN THAN BUILDING A BRIDGE OVER IT.

This is a world away from the fictional drama that played out in Pierre Boulle's internationally renowned novel *A Bridge over the River Kwai* – where prisoners of war were forced to build parts of the Burma Railway across the river in 1942–43. Instead, the FloatHouse is an oasis of peace and calm.

ARE WE GOING TO WAKE UP MILES DOWNRIVER?

The FloatHouse is tethered to the lush, wild jungle that spreads out behind the resort. In fact, the only way to get to the private rooms on The FloatHouse is to arrive by boat. If the absence of typical Southeast Asian traffic noise isn't enough to begin the destressing process, then step inside your private sanctuary decorated in traditional style and be soothed by the panoramic scenery from your private balcony and sundeck.

ONCE WE WAKE FROM OUR SOOTHING STUPOR, CAN WE GET OFF TO EXPLORE?

Absolutely. Private boats are available to ferry you to spectacular local attractions like hot springs, waterfalls, the Hellfire Pass, Lawa Cave and Mon Villages and temples, among others.

TOWN LITTLEWORTH, BARCOMBE, EAST SUSSEX, BN8 4TD, UK

WWW.THESECRETCAMPSITE.CO.UK

The Secret Campsite, Town Littleworth, East Sussex, UK

OH GO ON THEN, WE LOVE A SECRET. WE PROMISE WE WON'T TELL ANYONE.
Tucked away in a beautiful woodland meadow in a peaceful part of East Sussex, the large and secluded campsites each have their own fire pit and shared (free) hot showers.

WE DON'T MEAN TO BE RUDE BUT THIS JUST SOUNDS LIKE A REGULAR CAMPSITE.
There are a couple of little surprises. The first being an ingeniously designed Tree Tent. Suspended between three oak trees, the tent is accessed by wooden stairs and has views out over the South Downs National Park. The second secret treat is the six-person Gridshell, made from an ash structure covered in canvas. Both of these unique structures are available for rent and both come with their own outdoor fire pit for romantic fireside evenings. If you fall in love with either the Tree Tent or the Gridshell, the designer, Jason Thawley, takes commissions.

WHAT ABOUT THE AMENITIES INSIDE THE SPECIAL TENTS?
Mattresses are provided inside the tents. The Tree Tent sleeps two and the Gridshell sleeps six. Amenities are basic, but it's more about the beautiful secluded setting and peaceful communion with nature than it is about luxury.

EDEFORSVÄG 2 A, 960 24 HARADS, SWEDEN

WWW.TREEHOTEL.SE/EN/

Treehotel, Harads, Sweden

THIS PLACE LOOKS SO COOL WE DON'T KNOW WHICH TREE HOUSE TO CHOOSE.

We think you'll need to make a few trips. It's impossible to say which striking structure is the most impressive – is it the UFO, the Bird's Nest, or the Mirrorcube? Even the more traditional looking rooms, the Blue Cone, the Cabin, and the Dragonfly, are stunningly beautiful.

YOU'LL HAVE TO HELP US WITH THE DECISION.

Consider the UFO if you're bringing the kids along for the ride – it sleeps five and has a living area and bathroom. The Mirrorcube suits couples with its cool, classic Birchwood interior and romantic, rooftop terrace. We love the contrast of the Bird's Nest from its shambolic exterior of jumbled sticks to the spacious interior with two bedrooms, lounge room and bathroom.

WE COULDN'T HELP NOTICING THERE ARE NO KITCHENS.

A short walk away is Britta's Pensionat, where all guests of the Treehotel are welcome to come and enjoy a home-cooked breakfast, lunch and dinner. It is possible to have meals delivered to the privacy of your own room if you don't feel like socialising. Britta's also provides tree house guests with access to a bar, sauna, lounge area and TV.

Whitepod, Les Cerniers, Swiss Alps, Switzerland

IF ANYONE CAN ENGINEER DOMED ECO-PODS ON THE SIDE OF A MOUNTAIN IT'S THE SWISS.

There are 15 of these geodesic domes all loosely surrounding a wooden chalet that functions as a common room for guests of the domes. The geodesic design is durable, low impact and energy efficient; each Whitepod is heated by a small, wood-burning fire, and that's it.

SOUNDS PRETTY BASIC.

Simple but not basic. Rooms are modishly decorated with vintage skiing accoutrements, luxurious bedding and fully-equipped bathrooms. The central wooden chalet built in the 19th century has been modernised and is now set up for guests to socialise. This is where you'll find the breakfast room, a bar, sauna and massage area.

AND FOR OUTDOOR ACTIVITIES?

There's plenty to do in summer and winter. Summer sees the usually snow-covered slopes covered in wildflowers and criss-crossed with more than 25km of signposted hiking trails. In winter, look forward to skiing, snowboarding and sledding to your heart's content, before retiring to your cosy dome for the night.

Explore // Intrepid adventures

AV. EDUARDO RIBEIRO, 520 – SL. 304,
CENTRO, MANAUS – AM, BRAZIL
WWW.ANAVILHANASLODGE.COM

Anavilhanas Jungle Lodge, Manaus, Brazil

VISITING THE AMAZON RAINFOREST SHOULD BE ON EVERYONE'S BUCKET LIST.
Few places deliver a luxury Amazon experience quite like this. There are 22 private cabins divided up into 16 standard cottages, four superior bungalows and two top-of-the-range panoramic bungalows with, you guessed it, spectacular views.

WHAT'S THERE TO SEE IF WE VENTURE BEYOND OUR BEAUTIFUL CABIN?
Perched at the tip of an island in the Anavilhanas Archipelago, the largest freshwater archipelago in the world, the Jungle Lodge has a 13m-high observation deck with stunning views over the Rio Negro (there's a pretty good view from the pool too, just saying). If you're looking for adventure the lodge will organise a personalised itinerary so you can hike to local villages or take a boat tour around the tributaries, for example.

WILL OUR FOOTPRINT BE LIGHT IN THIS FRAGILE AND ENDANGERED AREA?
The lodge is sensitive to and conscious of its pristine surrounds. It is staffed almost exclusively by local people; there is no waste disposed of in the waters; preservation areas are strictly respected and they help to run social and educational programs with the help of the Brazilian government. All good.

Bivacco Gervasutti, Mont Blanc, Italy

THIS IS ONE FOR THE ADRENALINE JUNKIES, RIGHT?

It's fair to say that couch potatoes will want to settle for the pictures. The Bivacco Gervasutti perches precariously on the Frebouze Glacier on the Mont Blanc massif in Italy. Yes, that's Mont Blanc of the 'highest peak in Europe' fame.

WOW, THAT IS TOTALLY EXTREME.

Everything about this place is extreme. The striking red and white capsule, containing living and dining areas as well as two sleeping quarters for up to 12 people, cantilevers dramatically out over the cliff-face. From the inside it's like you're floating over the mountain. Solar panels keep the tube toasty year-round and there's even internet access so you can show off to your mates back home.

OK, HOW DO WE GET IN THERE?

That's the tricky bit: it's only accessible by foot. The architects of the structure were forced to build by helicoptering in one section at a time. There is no such luxury option for prospective guests. Only those who put in the hard graft to hike to the top reap the rewards of the spectacular views.

PUERTO NATALES, NATALES, MAGALLANES Y LA ANTÁRTICA
CHILENA REGION, CHILE. WWW.ECOCAMP.TRAVEL/EN

EcoCamp Patagonia, Torres del Paine National Park, Chile

CAMPING IN THE TORRES DEL PAINE SOUNDS AMAZING, BUT WON'T WE BE A BIT CHILLY?

This is where the genius of the geodesic dome comes in. Easy to erect, low-impact, and resistant to the elements, the EcoCamp has four different sizes of sleeping domes from standard (10m²) to Suite Dome Loft (37m²). Each dome is comfy and warm with wood-fire furnace and generous-sized beds with a small seating area. The domes have windows in the ceiling which are perfect for lazy stargazing at night.

FROM THE LOOKS OF THE SURROUNDINGS WE'RE GOING TO EARN OUR LUXURY FOR THE NIGHT.

The wild Patagonian plains are worthy of all the hyperbole. Guided treks from the EcoCamp will take you past snow-capped mountains, ancient forests, glacial lakes, gushing waterfalls and unique indigenous wildlife.

WE'RE BUILDING UP AN APPETITE.

The large community dome at the centre of camp serves up delicious meals in a relaxed and convivial environment. Perfect for sharing wilderness adventure stories with fellow trekkers.

P.O. BOX 1501, DK-3952 ILULISSAT, GREENLAND

HOTELARCTIC.COM

Hotel Arctic, Ilulissat, Greenland

IT'S NOT OFTEN THAT GREENLAND MAKES IT TO THE 'MUST-SEE' LISTS.

Remoteness and severe weather conditions put many travellers off making the trek this far north, but it is these very factors that make the Hotel Arctic so remarkable. The hotel sits right on the verge of the UNESCO World Heritage-Listed Ilulissat Ice Fjord.

WHAT'S SO AMAZING ABOUT THIS ICE FJORD?

The Ilulissat Ice Fjord contains one of the most fast-moving glaciers in the world, advancing over 20 metres every day. This rate of movement from a glacier that covers an area of approximately 3,000 square kilometres creates a spectacular natural phenomenon where inland ice is cleaved off and pressed out to sea. From your front-row seat at the Hotel Arctic you can witness a constantly moving and shifting landscape of glacial ice sculptures.

NO NEED FOR TV THEN.

If you can tear yourself away from the mesmerising landscape you'll find you're spoilt with a choice of luxury facilities and amenities in the hotel. Don't miss dining at the world-class Restaurant Ulo that specialises in dishes featuring locally foraged ingredients.

1860 BOULEVARD VALCARTIER, VALCARTIER, QUÉBEC, GOA,
450 CANADA. WWW.HOTELDEGLACE-CANADA.COM

Hotel De Glace, Québec, Canada

AREN'T WE OVER THE WHOLE ICE HOTEL/BAR THING?

As gimmicky as an ice hotel can seem from the outside there's nothing quite like spending a night encased in a room made entirely from exquisitely carved ice to stave off your scepticism.

ALRIGHT, WE'LL ASK THE OBVIOUS QUESTION: AREN'T WE GOING TO GET A LITTLE CHILLY?

The staff at the hotel are so confident of your comfort in the ice suites that their information sheet on staying the night recommends light clothing to sleep in to avoid getting too hot!

Each enormous ice slab is topped with a wooden wedge and a mattress to prevent you from shivering in your sleeping bag.

AND WHEN WE'RE NOT TUCKED UP IN BED?

There's a long list of suggested items of clothing to bring and wear during your stay to keep the cold at bay. That said, it's hard to imagine the cold creeping in when the surroundings are so spectacular. The Hotel De Glace is like one giant ice sculpture with individual suites designed in unique and magical themes. It's so beautiful it will warm the cockles of your heart.

Roar and Snore, Taronga Zoo, Sydney, Australia

DON'T WANT TO SEEM LIKE A SCAREDY CAT, BUT...

Relax, we wouldn't throw you to the lions. Instead, you'll be set up in fancy tents, just temptingly out of reach of the big cats, but as close to wildlife as is possible in the centre of Australia's largest city.

THE LAST THING WE EXPECTED FROM SYDNEY HARBOUR WAS A SAFARI.

Everyone knows the harbour's Opera House and iconic bridge, however, Taronga Zoo has also long been a favourite for Sydneysiders and out-of-towners alike; and it's easy to see why. Perched on the steep cliff-side of the northern harbour,

the zoo is accessed by cable car (or many, many, muscle-straining stairs) from the jetty at the water's edge. Once inside, a rambling path weaves past the enclosures, housing over 4000 animals from more than 350 different species.

SOUNDS AMAZING, SO WHY WOULD I COME HERE IN THE DARK?

Roar and Snore gives visitors the opportunity to get up close and personal with many of the zoo's inhabitants without competing with the crowds. Along with the ringside animal experience you'll receive snacks and drinks on arrival, a buffet dinner and breakfast before being allowed to roam the zoo the following day.

R342, PATERSON, 6130, SOUTH AFRICA

WWW.SHAMWARI.COM

Shamwari Game Reserve, Paterson, Eastern Cape, South Africa

AN AFRICAN SAFARI, THE STUFF OF DREAMS.
If this is the future of wildlife safaris, sign us up. Shamwari is an industry trailblazer and conservation crusader. The 25,000 hectare reserve has been painstakingly rejuvenated to a pristine state with flourishing flora and fauna. Its three education and rehabilitation facilities employ over 325 local staff, all so that the magnificent wildlife can roam free in their environment.

OK – TELL US ABOUT THE SAFARIS. THAT'S WHY WE'RE HERE.
There are numerous ways to get up close to the local wildlife, starting with the game drives and the guided walking safari.

Shamwari also arranges tours designed specifically for kids and a safari for professional photographers.

WE'RE WORN OUT. WHAT ARE THE SLEEPING ARRANGEMENTS LIKE?
The love and care put into conserving the environment for Africa's stunning wildlife is equalled by the attention to detail poured into the five-star accommodation onsite. There are six separate, luxury lodges. From the large 18-room Eagles Crag Lodge, to the Bayethe Tented Lodge with 12 detached tents, to the smaller six suite Villa Lobengula – every lodge option offers guests the utmost in indulgent amenities.

PISTA 224 KM, URUBAMBA-OLLANTAYTAMBO, CUSCO, PERU. WWW.ADVENTURE-LIFE.COM/PERU/SACRED-VALLEY/HOTELS/SKYLODGE-ADVENTURE-SUITES

Skylodge Adventure Suites, Cusco, Peru

WOW, JUST WOW.

We know, right! Who thought that clinging to the side of a mountain could be so relaxing? Installed in 2013, these cliff-side capsules are suspended over 1000 feet above the Sacred Valley floor in Peru. The combination of aluminium and polycarbonate as building materials mean that the capsules are almost completely see-through, which makes for gobsmacking views both day and night.

HOW ON EARTH DO YOU GET INTO THOSE THINGS?

Now that's the really wild part. You must either climb up the 1300-foot cliff (with the aid of steel ladders in parts) or hike the back route and hook on to a zip-line and swing in.

CAN WE EXPECT ANY CREATURE COMFORTS ONCE WE MAKE IT INSIDE?

We're pleased to report that you don't go unrewarded once making it to your bed for the night. Each of the three capsules hosts four beds, a dining area, and a private bathroom. There is solar-powered lighting and an open-air platform on top. You'll even receive a gourmet dinner with wine, and breakfast the next morning.

Splurge // High-end luxury

RANGALI ISLAND, RANGALI 20077, MALDIVES

WWW.CONRADMALDIVESRANGALI.COM

Conrad Maldives, Rangali Island, Rangali, Maldives

WITH A VIEW LIKE THAT, YOU DON'T NEED TO SAY ANYTHING.

Please indulge us – we may uncover even more gobsmacking tropical treats that you can't see.

WE'RE IN THE MALDIVES, SO WE'RE EXPECTING BEACHSIDE BLISS.

And that's exactly what you're going to get. The Maldives beaches are famous the world over for their crystalline waters, white sands and colourful underwater world. The Conrad Maldives supersizes this experience by offering guests a choice of over-the-water villas, luxury beachside bungalows or secluded waterside villas on the tiny island of Rangalifinolhu.

I THINK WE'RE JUST GOING TO MAKE OURSELVES AT HOME HERE ON OUR BEACHSIDE LOUNGER.

And why not? Views over such stunning waters and coral atolls are one in a million, but if for some crazy reason you manage to peel yourself from your waterside sunlounge, the resort also offers three spas, two pools, guided snorkelling tours with whale sharks, diving, and dolphin-spotting. Feeling peckish? There are 11 restaurants, including the see-to-be-believed Ithaa Undersea Restaurant. That's right, the whole dining room is encased in a plexiglass dome enabling you to dine as the spectacular tropical sea life swims overhead. A.M.A.Z.I.N.G.

271 HUKA FALLS RD, TAUPO 3377, NEW ZEALAND

WWW.HUKALODGE.CO.NZ

Huka Lodge, Taupo, New Zealand

IT SEEMS LIKE EVERY SQUARE INCH OF THIS COUNTRY IS A NATURAL WONDER.
I know, right? But if you get tired of parking your campervan at breath-taking sites alongside the roadside then how about soaking up a little luxury at the exclusive Huka Lodge. Honestly, it's magic. That's what you get with a mix of manicured grounds, spectacular wilderness, and five-star pampering.

CAN YOU MAGIC ME THERE NOW?

I'll try ... Huka Lodge sits on 17 acres of private grounds right on the edge of the powerful turquoise waters of the Waikato River, just upstream from the dramatically beautiful Huka Falls. A short drive in almost any directions will take you to snow-capped mountains, lush wilderness, or pristine lakes and streams. After a day of exploring nature's bounty you'll dive into the sweet, sweet luxury of your suite. Are you there yet?

ALMOST ... TELL ME MORE.

Did we mention the exclusivity? There are only 25 suites, dotted throughout the Huka Lodge grounds. Each one carries a certain opulent, colonial style, with grand French doors that open wide to take in the stunning surrounds. And when lying around in the lap of luxury gets boring, there's always the swimming pool, tennis courts, croquet and petanque courts, and the private spa pools. You're there now, aren't you?!

NIK. NOMIKOU (MAIN STREET), IA 847 02, GREECE

WWW.KATIKIESHOTELSANTORINI.COM

Katikies Hotel-Oia, Santorini, Greece

WHOAH, SUNGLASSES REQUIRED.
If you thought places like this were the stuff of Greek myth, think again. The blindingly beautiful contrast of blue and white is the stuff that holiday legends are made of.

ARE YOU SURE THIS PLACE HASN'T BEEN PHOTOSHOPPED?
The whitewashed walls of these cliff-side dream suites are typical of Cycladic architecture and certainly take a good picture but believe us, this is what it really looks like. Really.

THEN OUR TOUGHEST DECISION WILL BE BETWEEN DIVING INTO THE AZURE SEA OR FLOATING AROUND IN OUR PRIVATE PLUNGE POOL.
Well someone's gotta do it. There's also the option of having tired muscles pummelled or soothing beauty therapies applied at the onsite wellness centre. And then there's the difficult decisions to make at dinner time – will it be Byzantine-inspired meals at the Mikrasia Restaurant? Or perhaps see in the sunset at the Champagne Bar and Restaurant? If you can't drag yourself away from the infinity pool, you may just have to satiate your cocktail cravings poolside.

– 50 PLACES TO STAY TO BLOW YOUR MIND –

122ND MILESTONE, DELHI-JAIPUR HIGHWAY, VILLAGE NEEMRANA, DISTRICT ALWAR,
RAJASTHAN 301705, INDIA. WWW.FORT-PALACE.NEEMRANAHOTELS.COM

Neemrana Fort Palace, Rajasthan, India

THIS IS A PRETTY SPECIAL LOCATION.
Fit for a king. Built in the 15th century, the palace was dug into the hillside in order to provide both protection for the reigning monarch and stunning views over his land and subjects.

AND THESE DAYS?
In the late 1980s and early 1990s the Fort Palace was painstakingly restored, maintaining its authentic design and decorations in order to house guests. The hotel boasts 55 meticulously designed rooms boasting antiques and traditional Indian furniture. There are also two swimming pools, a spa and salon, an amphitheatre and a restaurant with outdoor seating that is lit with hundreds of fairy lights in the evening to create a magical environment.

IT CERTAINLY SOUNDS AS THOUGH WE'LL BE TREATED LIKE ROYALTY.
If the preening, pampering, and lying around the pool all day get to be too much the hotel can arrange some activities, like an early morning hot-air balloon ride, or perhaps you'd like a date with India's first zip-line – it careens across the Fort, giving guests a bird's eye view of the village below.

NO. 5858 TAIHU ROAD, HUZHOU, ZHEJIANG 313000, CHINA. WWW.STARWOODHOTELS.COM/
SHERATON/PROPERTY/OVERVIEW/INDEX.HTML?PROPERTYID=3414&LANGUAGE=EN_US

Sheraton Huzhou Hot Spring Resort, Huzhou, China

WE'VE SEEN SOME SPECTACULAR ARCHITECTURE IN OUR TIME BUT THIS ONE REALLY TAKES THE CAKE.

Hotel construction in China is like a national sport: each project is bigger and more out-of-this-world than the last. The Huzhou Hot Spring, affectionately coined 'The Donut', is the brainchild of Beijing-based architect Ma Yansong and features 321 rooms over 29 floors, 27 of which are above ground, two of which are below the water.

BELOW THE WATER?

Yep, that's right, the bottom part of this supersized structure is under the waters of Lake Taihu, giving the impression not so much of a donut, but of an enormous horseshoe rising spectacularly out of the lake.

SOUNDS LIKE NO EXPENSE HAS BEEN SPARED.

And we've only just begun. The lobby is lit by over 20,000 Swarovski crystal lamps, floors are paved in white jade and Tiger's Eye stone from Brazil. Hotel suites feature marble bathrooms with sunken baths and giant walk-in showers. Even the basic rooms have their own private balcony with expansive views over the lake. There are three restaurants, two cocktail lounges, a fully-equipped gym and two indoor pools. Opulence to the max.

HANSON BAY ROAD, KINGSCOTE SA 5223, AUSTRALIA

SOUTHERNOCEANLODGE.COM.AU

Southern Ocean Lodge, Kangaroo Island, Australia

JUST WHAT WE WERE EXPECTING FROM AUSTRALIA: A HOTEL BY THE BEACH.
Everyone knows about Australia's famous east and west coast beaches, their sun-kissed golden sands and tanned tourists jostling for space near the aquamarine water. This place is different. Right down south on the edge of the Great Southern Ocean the water is wild and the coastline rugged and windswept. There are no crowds, just you and the elements, oh – and five-star luxury.

SO JUST US AND THE KANGAROOS?
Kangaroo Island is home to much more than its well known namesake. More than a third of the island has been declared as either conservation area or National Park, so native species such as koalas, echidnas, wallabies, osprey and the ubiquitous kangaroo abound.

SOUNDS WILD.
If you're a creature that likes your comforts indoors then the Lodge won't disappoint. From your lavishly-appointed room, fitted with natural materials like limestone floors and feature walls made from spotted gum trees, there are uninterrupted views of the ocean. Sink into a king-sized bed or a couch in your sunken lounge and take in the wilderness from your own private piece of remote paradise.

SIRINYALI MAH. LARA 07160, ANTALYA, TURKEY

WWW.THEMARMARAHOTELS.COM/THE-MARMARA-ANTALYA-HOTEL.ASPX

The Marmara Antalya, Antalya, Turkey

WE'VE HEARD THIS PLACE IS ALSO KNOWN AS THE 'SPINNING HOTEL'.

Now before you get spooked by the nickname we'd say the hotel doesn't so much spin as gently rotate to give its guests continually changing views of the fabulous turquoise waters of the Antalyan Coast and the famous Falez Cliffs.

HOW IS THAT EVEN POSSIBLE?

A mammoth feat of engineering – the 2750-tonne revolving annex floats in a giant tank with close to 500 tonnes of water. A full rotation can take between two and 22 hours so you can say goodnight facing the pool and wake up with a stunning view across the sea.

NOW WE KNOW ALL ABOUT THE BUSINESS END, LET US IN ON THE PLEASURE.

The quirky design of this hotel isn't only in its external engineering. The Marmara Antalya prides itself on providing its guests with plenty to do – enter Tuti, part restaurant and part play centre for adults. The enormous space is dotted with giant columns all themed with entertainment in mind. There's a climbing column, a column that doubles as a library, one as a business centre, and one which you're free to graffiti. Lots of fun.

FIFTH AVENUE AT CENTRAL PARK SOUTH, NEW YORK,
NY 10019, USA. WWW.THEPLAZANY.COM

The Plaza, New York City, USA

OH SURE, THE PLAZA, YOU COULD BUY A CAR FOR THE PRICE OF A ROOM.

The Plaza definitely sits in the splurge category, no doubt. But everyone can dream, right? And if one day you do just happen to be on the receiving end of a windfall there are worse ways to get rid of money than a night in this New York icon of luxury and style.

WE'LL SUSPEND OUR DISBELIEF AND COME ALONG FOR THE RIDE.

Welcome to another world. Built in 1907, the Plaza was immediately celebrated as one of the most elegant and opulent hotels in the world. This reputation for sophisticated sumptuousness has never slipped, and was certainly in no danger of going south after the building received a $450 million facelift in 2008. The lure of luxury has long attracted the crème de la crème of NY society, as well as countless celebrities, dignitaries and even royalty.

IS THERE ANY WAY WE CAN FOLLOW IN THESE FOOTSTEPS WITHOUT SELLING OUR FIRSTBORN?

We're happy to report there are ways ordinary folk like us can get a Plaza experience. Try a tipple in the Oak Room, Rose Bar, or Champagne Bar, or wander the enormous Plaza Food Hall.

Wonder // The totally unexpected

DOKKADE 5, 8861KG, HARLINGEN, THE NETHERLANDS

WWW.HAVENKRAAN.NL

Crane Hotel, Harlingen, The Netherlands

WE TWIGGED THIS PLACE WAS UNUSUAL WHEN WE ARRIVED AT THE DOCKYARDS.
The real surprise is that we're sending you to the top of a fully functioning dockside crane for the night.

I FEEL MY FEAR OF HEIGHTS RISING.
This is not a dream destination for acrophobics, but the utilitarian essence of the crane has been reimagined for comfort with some truly inspired engineering and design.

WE'RE STILL NOT SURE WE WANT TO CLIMB 50 FOOT JUST TO GET INTO BED.
Step one of the process of redesigning the crane for hospitality purposes was to remove the external ladders and replace them with modern lifts. No sweat needed.

AND ONCE WE'RE IN?
Here's the truly special bit: the bedroom (which sleeps just two) is the former machine room, now luxuriously appointed with king-sized bed, flat-screen TV, computer-controlled temperature and lighting and, most dramatically, the ability to rotate for continuously changing views over the docks. Breakfast is delivered via the internal lift each morning, to be enjoyed on your private sundeck. Enough to make you forget all about your fear of heights.

Crazy Bear, Beaconsfield, Buckinghamshire, UK

SO WHAT'S ALL THIS THEN?

We imagine this is what it would look like if Alice fell down the rabbit hole marked 'Adults Only'. Crazy Bear Beaconsfield is so sumptuous and lavish that it all feels a bit naughty.

WE DIDN'T EXPECT TO FIND THIS IN RURAL BUCKINGHAMSHIRE.

The façade of the hotel, the oldest documented building in Beaconsfield, dating from the 15th century, only hints at the opulence inside. We think that the Crazy Bear Group, which has two other locations in Fitzrovia and Stadhampton, has a mission statement that aims to satisfy a modern-day Roman emperor. Interiors are a sexy mash-up of materials like velvet, brass, leather, marble and glass all dimly lit with glittering chandeliers and renaissance-style candelabras dripping with crystals. Bring your bon vivant self.

IS THERE A PLEBEIAN TO PEEL OUR GRAPES?

Better yet, your choice of two restaurants, old English and Thai. They feature such gastronomic pleasures as the confit belly of house-raised Old-Spot pork or whole native lobster with ginger, plum and a papaya salad, just two examples from menus that showcase over 100 dishes. Dress for excess.

FLINDERS STREET, 0886 JABIRU, AUSTRALIA. WWW.ACCORHOTELS.COM/
GB/HOTEL-9616-MERCURE-KAKADU-CROCODILE-HOTEL/INDEX.SHTML

Crocodile Hotel, Jabiru, Northern Territory, Australia

NOTHING SAYS ADVENTURE LIKE SLEEPING WITH THE CROCODILES, RIGHT?

As terrifying as Australia's saltwater crocodiles are to come across in the wilds of Kakadu National Park, this is one you won't mind meeting up close. The whole hotel is shaped like a gigantic saltwater croc. There's even a pool in the belly of the beast with rooms spread out around either side.

SOUNDS TOTALLY KITSCH.

There's an undeniably quirky edge to this place, but nothing tacky. The hotel is entirely indigenous-owned and there's a bush-tucker-inspired menu at the restaurant that features local ingredients like crocodile and kangaroo. Indigenous art adorns the walls in the rooms and there's even a small gallery which showcases indigenous art and sculpture.

WHEN WE'RE DONE LOUNGING AROUND THE POOL, CAN WE GET OUT INTO KAKADU?

The hotel is ideally located close to some of Kakadu's most stunning natural attractions, such as Cahill's Crossing, the Mamukala Wetlands and the Yellow Water Billabong. The staff will be more than happy to point you in the right direction or organise any tours you'd like to join.

RODLSTRARE 21, 4100 OTTENSHEIM, AUSTRIA

DASPARKHOTEL.NET

Das Park Hotel, Ottensheim, Austria

WE COULD BE WRONG, BUT ARE WE LOOKING AT SLEEPING IN ENORMOUS CONCRETE PIPES?

You're not wrong. In fact, they're enormous disused sewerage pipes. Still interested?

WE'RE ALL FOR RECYCLING, BUT SERIOUSLY.

Relax, do you really think we'd recommend you sleep in a literal shit hole? Of course not. The pipes are huge off-cuts from the materials used for sewerage systems under major cities. We promise they're clean.

OK, WELL OUR NEXT CONCERN IS LIGHT – CEMENT PIPES DON'T HAVE A REPUTATION FOR BEING WELL-LIT.

Very little has been done to the pipes to make them habitable, but small changes have managed to make a comfortable difference. Each pipe sports a circular sky light over a double bed, with a blanket and light cotton sleeping bag. The basic interiors have also been adorned with colourful painted murals.

WE HAVE TO ADMIT WE'RE COMING AROUND TO THE IDEA.

The unusual payment system might make up your mind. There is no set price, the pipes are rented out on a donation-only basis.

Hang Nga Guesthouse, Dalat, Vietnam

WE DON'T QUITE KNOW WHAT TO MAKE OF THIS.

You're not the only ones. Hang Nga Guesthouse is also known locally as 'the crazy house'.

SO WHAT'S THE DEAL?

The eponymous project, or should we say folly, of a quirky local architect, this is a tree house with a difference. Well, a considerable number of differences actually. For one, the body of the building is the tree as opposed to a structure being perched in the canopy of a tree. The additional building materials, which include concrete and stone, seem

to ooze into the spaces within the tree's branches. Rooms are across five levels and are accessed by ladders and twisted tunnels – it's a little bit Gaudi, a little bit Dalí, and a little bit Hobbit.

AND THE CRAZY BIT?

Have you been listening? If we haven't given you the impression that this place is one out of the box then here's some more examples of rampant eccentricity. There's a teahouse inside a giant giraffe, and themed rooms that feature exotic animals carved from stone. The monkey cage is surely, however, a step too far.

CALLE TORREA, I, ELCIEGO, 01340, SPAIN

WWW.HOTEL-MARQUESDERISCAL.COM/EN

Hotel Marques De Riscal, Elciego, Spain

BASQUE COUNTRY, VINEYARDS, MEDIEVAL TOWNSHIPS, WHAT MORE COULD WE WANT?
Sometimes a mind-blowing place to stay is about its location, sometimes its historical significance, and sometimes its architectural excellence. Rarely does a place tick all the boxes. Hotel Marques De Riscal is one such place, predominantly because it's the one and only hotel ever designed by architectural genius Frank Gehry, he of Guggenheim and Bilbao fame.

STRANGE SETTING FOR A PIECE OF POST-MODERN ARCHITECTURAL PERFECTION.
Rising dramatically from the rows of verdant vines is the unmistakable vision that is Gehry's work. Enormous metal ribbons flow in organic forms from the dramatic angles of the rest of the building, a breathtaking juxtaposition.

WE CAN'T WAIT TO SEE INSIDE.
As with all beautifully designed buildings the hotel's interior complements the exterior. Floor to ceiling windows zigzag at sharp angles letting in floods of light. The 43 individually dressed rooms are painted crisp white with wooden accents, they're sparingly furnished to make the most of the views. If you tire of marvelling at the surrounds there's a spa, restaurant and pool at your disposal.

Hotel Sidi Driss, Matmata, Tunisia

ONE FOR THE STAR WARS FANS?

Apologies to the Millennials for whom this might not mean so much, or for the 30-odd people out there who haven't ever seen the original *Star Wars* trilogy. This hotel was the setting of Luke Skywalker's childhood home on Tatooine. Many *Star Wars* scenes were filmed in the surrounding area and Hotel Sidi Driss featured as the home of Luke's Uncle Owen and Aunt Beru.

WHAT'S IN IT FOR US IF WE AREN'T INTO STAR WARS?

Even without the filmic significance of the location the hotel is a fascinating example of traditional Berber architecture, with rooms carved underground into the sandstone. Locally it's believed that the underground village of Matmata dates back to around 200 BC.

A 2000-YEAR-OLD CAVERN DUG UNDERGROUND? I'M GUESSING WE'RE ROUGHING IT.

Over the years the hotel has had periods of disrepair but the filming of *Star Wars: Attack of the Clones* in 2000 meant that the hotel was fully restored and now regularly features on tourists' itineraries. The hotel has 20 private rooms in four separate caverns; the fifth cavern is the hotel's restaurant.

HOBRECHTSTRAßE 66, 12047 BERLIN, GERMANY

WWW.HUETTENPALAST.DE

Huettenpalast, Berlin, Germany

NOT ANOTHER CONVERTED FACTORY WAREHOUSE.

We're going to hedge our bets and say you won't have seen one quite like this before. Sure, from the outside it's an old vacuum cleaner factory, but on the inside you'll see it has been turned into a whimsical indoor camping site fitted with renovated, retro caravans and wooden cabins as accommodation.

HOW CUTE.

As well as the charming caravans and cabins, the hotel serves breakfast by hanging little bags of croissants, fresh fruit and juice on a painted tree each morning for guests to collect and share in the common dining areas. There is an onsite café serving more substantial dishes if your foraged meal doesn't fill you up.

THE ONLY THING MISSING FROM THIS CAMPING EXPERIENCE IS THE OUTDOORS.

They've thought about that too. Outside there's a garden patio complete with shared seating so you can get to know your fellow campers, or hammocks for lounging around. And for a truly authentic camping adventure there are (clean) communal toilets and showers.

SHEIKH ZAYED ROAD, BUSINESS BAY, DUBAI 121000, UNITED ARAB EMIRATES

WWW.MARRIOTT.CO.UK/HOTELS/TRAVEL/DXBJW-JW-MARRIOTT-MARQUIS-HOTEL-DUBAI/

JW Marriott Marquis, Dubai, United Arab Emirates

IT'S HARD TO MISS THIS PLACE.

No wonder: it's currently the world record holder for tallest hotel, at a staggering 355m. Though something tells us it's not going to be a long time before an ambitious architect with multi-million-dollar backers makes a bid for the title, so get in quick if you like adding world record feathers to your bow.

HAS ALL THE EFFORT GONE INTO RECORD BREAKING?

You're not going to find a modern hotel such as this packed with character and charm, but that said there's a flamboyance and sense of style that a flagship hotel brings to the hospitality table. Guests will be spoiled with a bar, spa, steam room, fitness centre, outdoor heated pool, and stunning views of Burj Khalifa, the world's tallest building at 830m.

OH, THE BURJ KHALIFA MAKES US FEEL SMALL.

If you're in any doubt as to the astounding height of your hotel digs, take a ride in the elevator. Despite the obvious speed you're travelling at, it still takes an inordinate amount of time to get where you want to go.

IO, GREENLANDS LANE, COLOMBO 05, SRI LANKA

KUMBUKRIVER.COM

Kumbuk River Resort, Moneragala, Sri Lanka

SOMETHING TELLS US WE'RE IN FOR A UNIQUE EXPERIENCE.

What tipped you off? Was it the guesthouse shaped like a 40-foot elephant made of wood and straw?

THAT HAD SOMETHING TO DO WITH IT.

The striking structure is responsible for putting this river resort on the map. The comfortable villa has two bedrooms, a bathroom and an outdoor lounge area on the upper deck (that would be just behind the elephant's head). Not to be completely outshone, the other accommodation options are similarly unusual; for example, there's a luxury tree

house and a huge diesel lorry converted into a one-bedroom caravan.

SOUNDS LIKE A QUIRKY PLACE.

It's not all about the eccentric accommodation. This is a respected 16-acre eco-lodge that's positioned right on the edge of Sri Lanka's premier wildlife reserve, Yala. Expect to scale back your 21st-century lifestyle to the bare minimum – go swimming or fishing (or both) in the Kumbuk River; go hiking in the jungle; traverse the treetops by walking the suspension bridge; or just sit and enjoy the peace in such a remote and beautiful location.

Montana Magica Lodge, Huilo, Region de los Ríos, Chile

WHAT IS THIS PLACE?

You sound like you've never seen a hotel shaped like a volcano, with cascading water gushing from the peak over its vine-covered sides.

UM, WELL, YEAH.

Well, you're going to love that the only way to get here is to hike through the 300,000-acre Huilo-Huilo UNESCO biosphere reserve in Southern Chile, and once you arrive, the only way inside is to brave a rickety rope bridge.

THIS IS CRAZY.

A total folly, granted, but that's what makes it such fun. After a long day of hiking through the jungle and letting your inner Tarzan out on South America's longest zip line (it runs through the reserve at a height of 1500m) you can return to the hotel for a soak in a huge hot tub carved from tree trunks. We're not even joking.

WE CAN'T EVEN IMAGINE WHAT THE ROOMS MUST BE LIKE.

Although the jungle creeps, squawks, croaks, and buzzes around you, the rooms at Magic Mountain are mini oases of rustic, cosy charm. With wooden ceilings and floors, and seats made from tree trunks, it's like sleeping in a luxury tree house.

Palacio de Sal, Uyuni, Bolivia

SALT FLATS AS FAR AS THE EYE CAN SEE – WHERE ON EARTH ARE WE SLEEPING?

Ingeniously harnessing the natural materials at hand (Salar de Uyuni is the largest salt flat in the world), the Palacio de Sal has had its walls, floors, ceilings and even some furniture made from salt blocks. The 30 simply styled private rooms look like salt igloos, and come with en suite bathroom and central heating.

THIS HOTEL IS MAKING ME THIRSTY.

Despite its location, this Palace of Salt makes every effort to keep guests from being high and dry. There's a bar, common lounge and restaurant. The indulgent amenities even extend to a spa with sauna and steam room, and a salt water pool and whirlpool baths. A welcome relief after a day spent exploring the blindingly beautiful salt flats.

IS THAT A GOLF COURSE WE CAN SEE?

Not your usual spread of green, is it? From May to November the hotel opens a unique 9-hole golf course so you can smack balls across the hard surface of salt.

ALBRECHT-ACHILLES-STRAßE 58, 10709 BERLIN, GERMANY

WWW.PROPELLER-ISLAND.DE

Propeller Island City Lodge, Berlin, Germany

WE CANNOT FOR THE LIFE OF US WORK OUT WHAT THIS PLACE IS ABOUT FROM THE PICTURES.

You're not alone there. This hotel takes some explaining. It has to rank as one of the weirdest places where you can pay to spend a night.

OH COME ON, HOW STRANGE COULD IT BE?

How about sleeping under floorboards in a room that is entirely upside down? Or dozing off in a padded room designed to simulate a coffin? There's a room with walls entirely covered in angled mirrors, one with terraced beds sloped at different angles. Ever wondered what it would be like to go to jail? Then check out the Freedom room, kitted out just like a real prison cell.

WHOAH, THAT DOES SOUND WEIRD.

The hotel's philosophy is to 'alter your perspective on reality', so you might need to let go of your more traditional expectations of what a hotel room should be. Instead think of it more like sleeping inside an art installation. Still struggling? Request the Gallery Room, where the circular bed enclosed with strategically placed wooden frames continuously rotates to ensure a new perspective every few minutes.

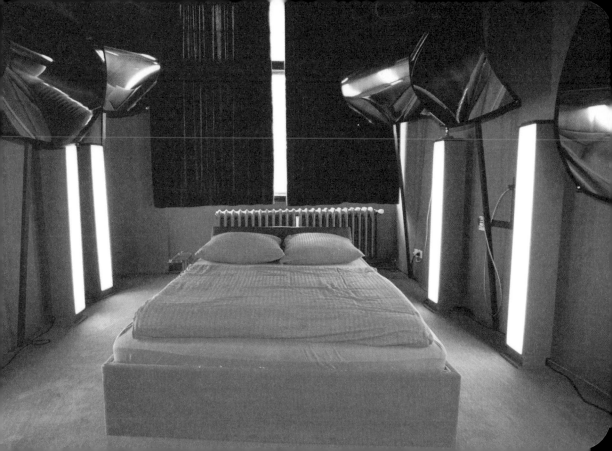

4-2-10, SHINJUKU, SHINJUKU-KU, TOKYO 160-0022, JAPAN

WWW.ANSHIN-OYADO.JP/ENGLISH/

Shinjuku Ekimae Anshin Oyado, Shinjuko, Tokyo

IS THIS A CAPSULE HOTEL? WE THOUGHT THEY WERE FULL OF BUSINESSMEN WHO ARE TOO DRUNK TO GET HOME FOR THE NIGHT.

Those capsule hotels do still exist, but this isn't one of them. You don't even have to be drunk to be welcomed here. On top of their relaxed door policy, this is a capsule hotel with services and amenities to rival its inner-city competitors with floor-space.

OK, SO WHAT DO WE GET TO GO WITH OUR HOLE IN THE WALL?

There's a spa with an artificial hot spring and mist sauna, massage chairs in the common area, and an Internet café with snacks like guri tea and pickled plums (there is also free Wi-Fi in the capsule itself). The rooms provide free products like shampoo, conditioner, cleanser, moisturising cream and slippers. Not bad for capsule prices.

AND ONCE WE CRAWL INTO OUR DRAWER SPACE?

Each capsule 'room' is equipped with LCD TV, quality headphones and superior bedding. And each floor is securely locked with an automatic system.

2421 BUSINESS LOOP HWY 95, COTTONWOOD, ID 83522, USA

WWW.DOGBARKPARKINN.COM

The Dog Bark Park Inn, Cottonwood, Idaho, USA

MUST LOVE DOGS?

It's not a prerequisite, but it certainly helps. This totally quirky bed and breakfast is housed inside the body of a 30-foot beagle. The belly of the beast sleeps two in a queen-sized bed, and a couple more guests can cosy up on twin beds in the beagle's head. It almost goes without saying that the décor is doggy-inspired.

WE MAY REGRET ASKING THIS QUESTION, BUT HOW DO YOU GET INSIDE?

Let's just say, at this laid-back little place, you use the back door. Ahem, next question.

WE CAN'T DECIDE IF THIS IS GENIUS OR COMPLETELY BONKERS.

Why not let your best friend decide. 'Responsible pets and their well-behaved humans' are more than welcome, say the B&B's owners, husband and wife team Dennis and Frances.

WHERE DO ALL THESE CARVED WOODEN DOG SCULPTURES COME FROM?

When Dennis and Frances aren't baking fresh pastries for their guests' breakfast they're outside carving dogs out of wood with a chainsaw. Sculptures are available for purchase and it's even possible to request a bespoke piece in the likeness of your own unique pooch.

Tianzi Garden Hotel, Hebei, China

THIS PLACE MIGHT TAKE SOME EXPLAINING.

It's fair to say that the Tianzi makes it on to 'Most Unusual' lists more than anything else. It's not every day you run across a 10-storey high edifice built both to house guests and resemble a trio of Chinese deities.

WE'RE SPEECHLESS, BUT PLEASE EXPLAIN.

The three gentlemen represented in kaleidoscopic colour are known as Fu, Lu and Shou – the Chinese gods of fortune, prosperity and longevity. The entrance to the hotel is through Shou's shoe (he's the guy with the long white beard) and he also happens to be holding the hotel's best suite in the palm of his hand, otherwise known as the Peach of Immortality.

IS THERE ANYTHING ELSE TO DO ONCE WE'RE DONE OGLING THE ODDITY?

To be completely honest, no. The towering gods are the only real drawcard out here in Beijing's semi-industrial suburbs. The hotel itself is mostly surrounded by power plants and ordinary apartment blocks. Not likely to make it on to any beaten tourist trail any time soon.

GRAF-ZEPPELIN-PLATZ I, 71034 BÖBLINGEN, GERMANY

WWW.V8HOTEL.DE

V8 Hotel, Boblingen, Stuttgart, Germany

LADIES AND GENTLEMEN, PLEASE START YOUR ENGINES.

Indeed. If your love of cars borders on extreme, then this place takes your fantasies to the next level. Deep breaths, rev-heads: you're about to be very happy, because rooms at this one-of-a-kind hotel are entirely themed around the automobile, from classic and vintage cars to racing cars, and even the motors of the future.

PUTS A NEW SPIN ON THE CONCEPT OF A DRIVING TRIP.

There's no hiding the purpose of your trip; this is Stuttgart's Motorworld region. It's all about cars, cars and more cars.

MOTOR ENTHUSIASTS CAN BE A PERNICKETY LOT; I HOPE V8 KNOWS ITS STUFF.

No detail has been overlooked. The rooms feature genuine parts and striking images from the automotive industry. In some cases, the beds are actually part car. For a top-of-the-line splurge, try the Mercedes suite which, as well as providing a vintage, silver Mercedes sedan fashioned as an enormous bed, also gives you access to a private rooftop terrace and second floor bathroom with private sauna.

About the author

Kalya Ryan loves an excuse to sleep in a hotel for the night, and even though she's not likely to see some of the more opulent examples of a place to rest your head, she likes to dream. If the opportunity ever arose it's the Free Spirit Spheres that tickle her fancy.

Index

Africa

Asia

© CRAZY BEAR, © THE DOG BARK PARK INN

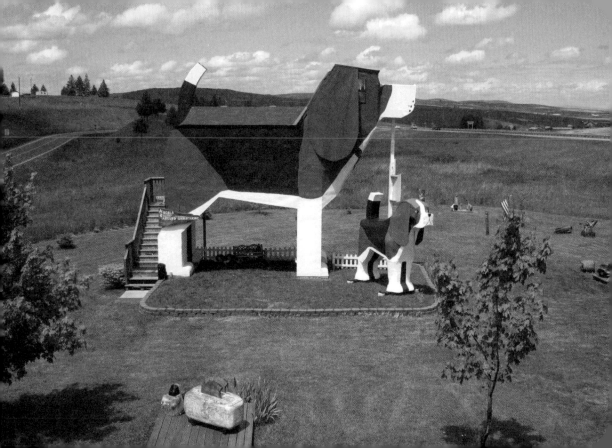

PILAR OLIVARES © REUTERS. © 2015 RICHARD MANDELKORN

Europe

North America

Oceania

South America

More things to blow your mind

50 Bars to Blow Your Mind

Lonely Planet handpicks the world's most extraordinary drinking holes, from caverns and island party havens to a bar nestled in an ancient tree trunk.
ISBN 978-1-76034-058-2

50 Museums to Blow Your Mind

Whether you're a history buff, tech-head or have an inexplicable fascination with clowns, you'll find world-class collections here to pique your interest.
ISBN 978-1-76034-060-5

50 Beaches to Blow Your Mind

Discover the planet's most pristine, jaw-dropping, wild and wonderful sandy spots.

ISBN 978-1-76034-059-9

50 Natural Wonders to Blow Your Mind

A tour of the world's most wild and wonderful places: discover just how extraordinary our planet really is.
ISBN 978-1-78657-406-0

50 Festivals to Blow Your Mind

Whatever you like to celebrate, you'll find a gathering somewhere on the planet to suit you. Find the greatest festivals for you to set your sights on.
ISBN 978-1-78657-404-6

Published in May 2017 by Lonely Planet
Global Limited
CRN 554153
www.lonelyplanet.com
ISBN 978 1 78657 405 3
© Lonely Planet 2017
Printed in China
10 9 8 7 6 5 4 3 2 1

Written by **Kalya Ryan**
Managing Director, Publishing **Piers Pickard**
Associate Publisher **Robin Barton**
Commissioning Editor **Jessica Cole**
Art Direction **Daniel Di Paolo**
Layout Designer **Austin Taylor**
Editor **Kate Turvey**
Picture Researcher **Christina Webb**
Print Production **Larissa Frost, Nigel Longuet**
Cover image Kakslauttanen © Valtteri
Hirvonen

Lonely Planet offices

STAY IN TOUCH lonelyplanet.com/contact

AUSTRALIA The Malt Store, Level 3, 551
Swanston St, Carlton, Victoria 3053
03 8379 8000

IRELAND Unit E, Digital Court, The Digital
Hub, Rainsford St, Dublin 8

USA 150 Linden St, Oakland, CA 94607,
510 250 6400

UNITED KINGDOM 240 Blackfriars Rd,
London SE1 8NW, 020 3771 5100